Travel Journal
My Trip to South Africa

Copyright

Version 1
Copyright © 2014 Travel Diary
All rights reserved.
ISBN: 978-1-304-84117-9

Personal Details

Name: _____

Passport No. _____

Nationality: _____

DOB: _____

Address: _____

_____

Mobile No: _____

Email address: _____

Important Contact Information

Emergency No. _____

Insurance Co. _____

Insurance Number _____

Airline _____

Airline No. _____

Accommodation _____

Address _____

_____

Other Information _____

_____

Things to Pack

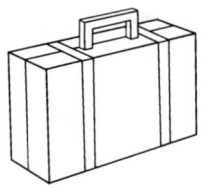

- ⭘ Tickets
- ⭘ Passport
- ⭘ Insurance Documents
- ⭘ Money
- ⭘ Travelers Checks
- ⭘ Credit Cards
- ⭘ Driver's License
- ⭘ Chargers
- ⭘ Batteries
- ⭘ Book to read
- ⭘ Kindle
- ⭘ Camera
- ⭘ Cell Phone
- ⭘ Ipad / tablet
- ⭘ Contact Lenses

- ⭘ Snacks
- ⭘ Toiletries
- ⭘ Towel
- ⭘ Umbrella
- ⭘ Water bottle
- ⭘ Walking shoes
- ⭘ Coat
- ⭘ Guide Books
- ⭘ Travel Journal
- ⭘ Hair Drier
- ⭘ Jewelry
- ⭘ Watch
- ⭘ Sun glasses
- ⭘ Sun cream
- ⭘ Medicine

Who I want to send postcards to, while I am away

Name: _____

Address: _____

Name: _____

Address: _____

Name: _____

Address: _____

Name: _____

Address: _____

Holiday Planner

Day

1 _____

_____

2 _____

_____

3 _____

_____

4 _____

_____

5 _____

_____

6 _____

Holiday Planner

Day

7 _____

_____

8 _____

_____

9 _____

_____

10 _____

_____

11 _____

_____

12 _____

Holiday Planner

Day

13 _____

_____

14 _____

_____

Notes

_____

_____

_____

_____

Record of Expenses

Item Bought	Price
Total	

See page 109 for useful information to help while shopping

Day 1Date

Weather: _____

Plan for the day

_____

_____

_____

_____

_____

Things we need to bring

_____

_____

_____

Diary of the Day

Memories of the Day

Places we liked

_____

_____

_____

People we met

_____

_____

Food we enjoyed

_____

_____

Things we bought

_____

_____

Day 2 _____   Date _____

                                      Weather: _____

Plan for the day

_____

_____

_____

_____

_____

Things we need to bring

_____

_____

_____

Diary of the Day

Memories of the Day

Places we liked

_____

_____

_____

People we met

_____

_____

Food we enjoyed

_____

_____

Things we bought

_____

_____

Day 3Date

Weather: _____

Plan for the day

_____

_____

_____

_____

_____

Things we need to bring

_____

_____

Diary of the Day

Memories of the Day

Places we liked

_____

_____

_____

People we met

_____

_____

Food we enjoyed

_____

_____

Things we bought

_____

_____

Day 4 _____   Date _____

Weather: _____

Plan for the day

_____

_____

_____

_____

_____

Things we need to bring

_____

_____

_____

Diary of the Day

Memories of the Day

Places we liked
_____
_____
_____

People we met
_____
_____

Food we enjoyed
_____
_____

Things we bought
_____
_____

Day 5   Date

Weather: _____

Plan for the day

_____

_____

_____

_____

_____

Things we need to bring

_____

_____

_____

Diary of the Day

Memories of the Day

Places we liked
_____
_____
_____

People we met
_____
_____

Food we enjoyed
_____
_____

Things we bought
_____
_____

Day 6   Date

Weather: _____

Plan for the day

_____

_____

_____

_____

_____

Things we need to bring

_____

_____

_____

Diary of the Day

Memories of the Day

Places we liked

_____

_____

_____

People we met

_____

_____

Food we enjoyed

_____

_____

Things we bought

_____

_____

Day 7　　　　　Date

Weather: _____

Plan for the day

_____

_____

_____

_____

_____

_____

Things we need to bring

_____

_____

_____

Diary of the Day

Memories of the Day

Places we liked

_____

_____

_____

People we met

_____

_____

Food we enjoyed

_____

_____

Things we bought

_____

_____

# Day 8 			Date

	Weather: _____

Plan for the day

_____

_____

_____

_____

_____

_____

Things we need to bring

_____

_____

_____

Diary of the Day

Memories of the Day

Places we liked

_____

_____

_____

People we met

_____

_____

Food we enjoyed

_____

_____

Things we bought

_____

_____

Day 9   Date

Weather: _____

Plan for the day

_____

_____

_____

_____

_____

Things we need to bring

_____

_____

_____

Diary of the Day

Memories of the Day

Places we liked

_____

_____

_____

People we met

_____

_____

Food we enjoyed

_____

_____

Things we bought

_____

_____

Day 10   Date

                         Weather: _____

Plan for the day

_____

_____

_____

_____

_____

Things we need to bring

_____

_____

_____

Diary of the Day

Memories of the Day

Places we liked

_____

_____

_____

People we met

_____

_____

Food we enjoyed

_____

_____

Things we bought

_____

_____

Day 11   Date

                     Weather: _____

Plan for the day

_____

_____

_____

_____

_____

Things we need to bring

_____

_____

_____

Diary of the Day

Memories of the Day

Places we liked

_____

_____

_____

People we met

_____

_____

Food we enjoyed

_____

_____

Things we bought

_____

_____

Day 12   Date _____

                 Weather: _____

Plan for the day

_____

_____

_____

_____

_____

Things we need to bring

_____

_____

_____

Diary of the Day

Memories of the Day

Places we liked

_____

_____

_____

People we met

_____

_____

Food we enjoyed

_____

_____

Things we bought

_____

_____

Day 13   Date

Weather: _____

Plan for the day

_____

_____

_____

_____

_____

Things we need to bring

_____

_____

_____

Diary of the Day

Memories of the Day

Places we liked

_____

_____

_____

People we met

_____

_____

Food we enjoyed

_____

_____

Things we bought

_____

_____

Day 14   Date

Weather: _____

Plan for the day

_____

_____

_____

_____

_____

Things we need to bring

_____

_____

_____

Diary of the Day

Memories of the Day

Places we liked

_____

_____

_____

People we met

_____

_____

Food we enjoyed

_____

_____

Things we bought

_____

_____

Things I will remember from our trip

_____

_____

_____

_____

_____

_____

_____

_____

_____

Enjoy Your Trip

Useful Information - Women

Women's Clothing Sizes							
UK	US	Japan	France, Spain & Portugal	Germany & Scandinavia	Italy	Australia & New Zealand	
6/8	6	7-9	36	34	40	8
10	8	9-11	38	36	42	10
12	10	11-13	40	38	44	12
14	12	13-15	42	39	46	14
16	14	15-17	44	40	48	16
18	16	17-19	46	42	50	18
20	18	19-21	48	44	52	20

Women's Shoe Sizes			
UK	European	US	Japanese
3	35 ½	5	22 ½
3 ½	36	5 ½	23
4	37	6	23
4 ½	37 ½	6 ½	23 ½
5	38	7	24
5 ½	39	7 ½	24
6	39 ½	8	24 ½
6 ½	40	7 ½	25
7	41	9 ½	25 ½
7 ½	41 ½	10	26
8	42	10 ½	26 ½

Useful Information – Men

Men's Suit / Coat / Sweater Sizes		
UK / US / Aus	EU /Japan	General
32	42	Small
34	44	Small
36	46	Small
38	48	Medium
40	50	Large
42	52	Large
44	54	Extra Large
46	56	Extra Large

Men's Pants/Trouser Sizes (Waist)	
UK / US	European
32	81 cm
34	86 cm
36	91 cm
38	97 cm
40	102 cm
42	107 cm

Men's Shoe Sizes			
UK	European	US	Japan
6	38 ½	6 ½	24 ½
6 ½	39	7	25
7	40	7 ½	25 ½
7 ½	41	8	26
8	42	8 ½	27 ½
8 ½	43	9	27 ½
9	43 ½	9 ½	28
9 ½	44	10	27 ½
10	44	10 ½	28 ½
10 ½	44 ½	11	29
11	45	12	29 ½

Useful Information for Kids

Children's Clothing Sizes			
UK	European	US	Australia
12 m	80 cm	12-18 m	
18 m	80-86 cm	18-24 m	18 m
24 m	86-92 cm	23/24 m	2
2-3	92-98 cm	2T	3
3-4	98-104 cm	4T	4
4-5	104-110 cm	5	5
5-6	110-116 cm	6	6
6-7	116-122 cm	6X-7	7
7-8	122-128 cm	7 to 8	8
8-9	128-134 cm	9 to 10	9
9-10	134-140 cm	10	10
10-11	140-146 cm	11	11
11-12	146-152 cm	14	12

Children's Shoe Sizes			
UK	European	US	Japan
4	20	4 ½ or 5	12 ½
4 ½	21	5 or 5 ½	13
5	21 or 22	5 ½ or 6	13 ½
5 ½	22	6	13 ½ or 14
6	23	6 ½ or 7	14 or 14 ½
6 ½	23 or 24	7 ½	14 ½ or 15
7	24	7 ½ or 8	15
7 ½	25	8 or 9	15 ½
8	25 or 26	8 ½ or 9	16
8 ½	26	9 ½	16 ½
9	27	9 ½ or 10	16 ½ or 17
10	28	10 ½ or 11	17 ½
10 ½ or 11	29	11 ½ or 12	18 or 18 ½
11 ½	30	12 ½	18
12	31	13	19 or 19 ½
12 ½	31	13 or 13 ½	19 ½ or 20
13	32	1	20
13 ½	32 ½	1 ½	20 ½
1	33	1 ½ or 2	21
2	34	2 ½ or 3	22

CPSIA information can be obtained at www.ICGtesting.com
Printed in the USA
BVOW05s1707240215

389109BV00003B/141/P